Write A Journal
So Your Soul Smiles

Dr. Melba Burns

Published by Soul Writes Books
Vancouver, B.C. Canada

Write a Journal So Your Soul Smiles

Published by Soul Writes Books

April 2014

Cover and book interior designed by Eve Lees

633 Bucket Wheel Place
Vancouver, British Columbia
Canada V5Z4A7

ISBN: 978-1-927497-01-2

"If you always imagined writing a journal but didn't know how to start, this is the book for you. Read it and begin an inner journey that will nourish you through your life. You won't find a better coach."

Deb Cameron-Fawkes, Writer, Theologian, Activist

"Whether you're a seasoned journal writer or someone who wants to try it out for the very first time, this book provides inspiration and guidance to that unique inner voice that lives within each of us. Like a wholesome meal, the chapters are short and easy to digest, with only the freshest ingredients that come from an authentic source. Melba Burns' own life experiences and her insightful processing style is why this book is a must-have in the kitchen of feeding one's own soul."

Maret Christiansen, Writer

Contents

I dedicate this book to You . . .

Wise person

Who wants to know

More about yourself.

May you find her

Through contemplation, examination

And writing

In your own journal.

Preface

Dear Reader

 s I wrote this book for you, I came from many years of my own journal writing. It has been my companion, my friend, and I have truly trusted the guidance received from the process of pen on page; the power of it as communion and direction from soul. As you read Write a Journal So Your Soul Smiles, my intention is for you to also receive a deep connection with Self. I know, first-hand, that when you write, your soul smiles.

You will receive many benefits:

No matter what you are experiencing in your life, your journal will lead you through the valley of dark like a hand guiding you, and the light will always appear. It may be just a glimmer some days, but as you continue to write, you'll see it and be led to joy and love.

Your journal will help you to see situations more clearly. It will keep you in integrity with your values, and give you the opportunity to actually know what they are by writing

1

them. It will provide space to think deeply about subjects that require reflection: to assess talents, dreams and meaning in your life.

You will learn that you don't have to depend upon anyone else. It will teach you self-reliance and discipline – just to show up at the page and address what is going on within.

Your journal pages will help guide your life so it evolves like a beautiful tapestry, with many textures, colors, and patterns. As you read through your own weavings, you will recognize how you have transformed: how your challenges have lifted you up so you've lived well; how you've navigated through turbulent times, survived – and thrived!

Trust your fingers to write from your heart. Trust your Self to keep you in integrity. Trust that when you spend time with your journal, your energy rises higher and your life expands in unimaginable ways. When you write in your journal you give a gift to your self. Let yourself receive it, for as you do, your soul will smile. Remember . . .

"It is never too late to be what you might have been."

— *George Eliot*

Sincerely,
Melba Burns, Ph.D.

Introduction

"For any writer who wants to keep a journal,
be alive to everything..." — May Sarton

 o you not write to hear yourself? Do you not write to draw forth whatever is lingering within you?

Do you not write to tune into a sweet place that is often left untended, like a beautiful plant un-watered? Like a limb that is stiff from un-use? You are tending your inner garden when you venture within, no matter what comes onto the page. Perhaps you have been longing for this soul-connection, just so you remember...

When you remember who you are, why you came here, what your purpose is, you can become a light in this world. The truth is that you were born with a spark in your eyes, but some of that diminished early on in life. If you are conscious of this, you can rekindle the spark; blow upon it, ignite embers so they fan into a bright flame, one that grows and illuminates your way. In doing this, you become a way-shower to others who have dimmed their own light. Then, your world brightens, filled with grace, and can evolve into a world of peace.

Within the twenty-three chapters of this book, there are over 270 questions to open you up to write, so you become clearer about various aspects of your life. Please don't feel you have to do these in order, but choose whatever appeals to you.

To help you to dive deeper into your soul, I have included several entries from my own journals, such as dialogues with my higher Self, poems and personal writings, so you have direct examples for many of the suggested topics.

Writing a journal will nudge your soul to smile. Remember though, that this is your book, to assist you in rediscovering and loving yourself – to empower you to be the greatest person you can be.

1

How to Start?

"Be yourself; everyone else is already taken."
— Henry David Thoreau

1. Choose a journal that feels comfortable, one that is not too fancy because you'll never put your worst thoughts in it. A Mead notebook, 8 X 11, has a plasticized cover which doesn't bend when you write in it. Three holes are punched into it so those pages can be put into a three-ring binder – to keep a whole year's worth of your writing. Yes, it is possible to type a journal onto your computer, but in my experience, writing by hand will enable you to go deeper within self.

2. Get yourself a good pen. The jelled pens flow smoothly over the pages. Buy a pen where you don't have to press too hard or wear yourself out in the writing with it.

3. Embrace your journal as if it is your best friend. It will become so because you will begin to write entries you have probably never told a soul. Talk to the pages as if you're talking to a dear friend. Write anything and your journal will keep your secrets. What a great feeling to know that everything will be held in confidence.

4. Allow your pen to write whatever thoughts come to your mind – no matter if they sound stupid, unkind, silly or unspeakable. This is your book and you can put into it whatever you feel like saying. Why? Because you will express what's *really* going on. So, rather than shutting down those old thoughts, suppressing them and stuffing them back into the ethers of your subconscious mind, here in your beloved journal you get to express them. Whew! What a relief to get them out of your mind! Do not edit. They don't have to make sense. This journal is just for you. Give yourself permission to be wild and passionate! Let your imagination take off into visions of what you'd really like to do in your life.

5. What if you don't have anything to say? Then, describe the weather, or your mood. Or what your eyes rest upon: A coffee cup, a photo, a pair of old socks, a beautiful vase; a favorite book –whatever. Just pick up your pen, hold on,

and allow it to flow onto the page. You will be surprised at what comes out. Write out this phrase: *What does my soul want to say today?* You'll soon discover that your soul may be smiling.

6. What if you don't want your partner or anyone to read it? Lock it up in your desk. Or, tuck it into a pillow case in your linen closet. Buy a little safety-deposit box and use that. Ask your partner for respect; tell him/her that this is a private thing. Tuck it into a file in your filing cabinet and give it a strange name. It is crucial that you feel safe with what you express.

Years ago, when I was 16, my mother wanted to know what was going on with my boyfriend and me, so she cut the lock on my diary and read it! As a parent, that may have been her protective prerogative, and now I can understand her invasion of my privacy, but I did not write in a journal for many years after that. So, please make sure you put it into a safe place – otherwise you won't express yourself from a depth that will help you to grow.

Now, of course, every day I write in my journal, and my soul smiles.

"When I sit down at my writing desk, time seems to vanish. I think it's a wonderful way to spend one's life."

— *Erica Jong*

2

Why Write in Your Journal?

"Isn't it mysterious to begin a new journal like this?
I can run my fingers through the fresh clean pages
but I cannot guess what the writing on them will be."
— Maud Hart Lovelace, Betsy in Spite of Herself.

*E*verything you do in your life deserves the question WHY, so here are a few responses to "Why write in your journal?"

1. It becomes your best friend; you can tell it anything. You get to dump any thoughts resounding through your head, without feeling foolish; nobody gets to read these but you, and as you write them, you feel closer to your self. *Dump any thoughts you have today into your journal.*

2. It is a mirror of where you are on a particular day.

Within a year or two, you can compare your experiences about a specific day; discover patterns. *Where are you today? What are you feeling?*

3. Perhaps you've just retired and have no idea about what you want to do with your life. Your pen in your journal will guide you because your words come from a deep place and will lead you on. They will lead you out of the rut of habitual days, to walk onto a new path with a clearer sense of your soul's journey. Lurking in the shadows of a too busy life, you will find your Self. Ask: *What would I like to do with my one beautiful life now that I am retired?*

4. It becomes a spiritual practice, and opens you to depths you have ignored. You learn discipline and perseverance when sticking to this practice. One day, amidst the chaos and tumult of your life, you will discover a shimmering thread. Follow it and find out where it is leading you – out and into a new way of being. *Where is your life's thread today?*

5. It clears your mind, provides a structure for your day. Your focus will sharpen for what is important. *Write out what you wish to do – then feel the satisfaction as you check off those points later on.*

6. It gives you a space, a container, to play with possibilities; things you might not ever mention to anyone, you can write them here. In your journal you can be wild and crazy and allow imagination to take off into visions of what you really want to do. *Write some of those possibilities now.*

7. When you write out your experiences of loving moments, reach further into your soul to describe them, you may find poetry splashing onto the page. *Write out a loving moment now.*

8. You get to document events, like having a hip replacement, or losing your lover. Rather than just struggling, unsupported, through these difficult times, writing about them will assuage the pain. You may even have a book to share. For example: When the love of my life left, penning poems from the hurt in my heart helped me create Love Leaves. *Start documenting your own challenges.*

9. When you venture in deep and write from those younger aspects of yourself, like your little child, you may start to unravel the threads that wove into patterns; some of them unhealthy. Some may have led you to the "wrong" partners;

they were so easy to fall in love with because they were comfortable and familiar. If you write these and bring them to the surface, you will understand, have compassion for your self, and not need to seek solace "out there," or in your lover's arms, but in your own. So you can make better choices and live a more conscious life – where you bring forth all you were meant to be rather than just being an extension of someone else. *Write how this applies to you now.*

10. Writing in your journal gives your soul time, freedom and feedback to let you know if you are in integrity with your values – or not. There's no judgment, no criticism, only your joy and delight as you feel your self expanding. *Write how you are expanding, or not.*

Engaging with your journal gives you courage to write things you have always wanted to express. By practicing in this private book, you gain a sense of what those ideas are; truth statements that need more expression in your world, philosophies, rants or raves – so you get to know what you are passionate about and what you could contribute to a larger audience to really make a difference in the world. In writing these words, your soul will find more meaning, and smile!

3

Make Time

"Life isn't about finding yourself. Life is about creating yourself." — George Bernard Shaw

1. Make Time to write in your journal. Make a date with yourself – and keep that date. I write in the morning because my thoughts are fresh then; that time becomes a lovely habit, like brushing my teeth or taking a shower. Your soul will thank you for this and you will look forward to that sacred time.

2. Date every entry so you can reference how you were feeling or what you did that day.

3. Write about what you did yesterday and how you *feel* about that. Please don't forget your feelings.

4. Write about what you are going to do today – and include your feelings about that. Are you experiencing joy and delight

as you write this, or annoyance and sadness? Through your writing, you will get to examine how you are living your life, and start to see how you'd like to live differently.

5. Write about the dream you had last night. Then, analyze it right there in your journal. Write about what it means to you now. It's amazing the guidance received from dreams.

6. Write to remind yourself that you are important. Enjoy the TIME you spend with yourself. For example: *I'm just catching the moment here before the phone starts ringing with an appointed call. Oh, where is this lovely day disappearing to? I have ideas to write, but no time.* Ever feel this way? So, what can you do about it? At least jot down what comes quickly and you can catch up later in the evening. Or, if it's related to an article you might wish to write, put it into a file called *Will Finish Later.*

7. Write about the frustrations of fitting your writing into your daily mix. How to do that?

Here are some ideas . . .

* Get up earlier so you can write first thing, before your phone rings – before you open your emails.

* Make dates with yourself: Make mornings your writing time – or choose a particular time and stick to it. Soon your friends will learn this about your writing habit, and you will actually inspire them to make dates with their own artist-self. When you make dates with people you honor them, don't you? So, why wouldn't you honor time with yourself?

* Even if you only have a few minutes, just jot the ideas down. Maybe your friend hasn't called yet, but you can get more written than you'd anticipated. Your writing-time matters and it will inspire others.

* Timing is always perfect. Trust that. Often, when someone else is late in showing up, you get a chance to do something you've been wanting to do: like read that article in the paper, write in your journal, write a poem, or just stare off into space like you used to do in grade four. Daydream!

* Take your notebook with you – wherever you go! You can always transfer those thoughts onto your computer back home.

8. Take time to regenerate and ask what is going on within: Quiet time is good for your soul and you get to tap into what has been hiding beneath the surface of your consciousness, disturbing your sleep and making you feel weepy and restless.

So, when you get quiet and ASK what is going on, you will be given truths you never knew were simmering there, and usually they will reveal more of yourself to you.

For_example: *I ask, what has been simmering under the surface of my insomnia?*
* Lots of sadness. A friend's partner just died and that reminds me of other loved ones who passed away just three months ago.
* Feeling my own sense of mortality.
* Fear that I will never get my books out there!
* Not liking ageing. It's no fun and sometimes when my body aches, I feel angry. Well, I don't want to feel that way about what is happening to me. Rather, I want to accept it for whatever it is – and acknowledge myself for still being in the game.

Remember this: You weren't given the gift and the talent to write unless it was also meant to be read – by you. Read your entries over and you will really learn more about yourself. They are dialogues with your self. When you are writing, you're letting go, but when you read them over, you "get" what's going on within. Someday, you may be ready to put some of them into a book – but <u>only</u> when you feel ready. Keep at it – no matter what.

Enjoy whatever time you give to yourself. You are important. Do you often forget that? Don't. You <u>are</u> important and your words matter; to the one who wrote them, and eventually, to others.

Can you feel your soul smiling? Yes, you are reclaiming that sacred aspect of you.

*"As far as we can discern, the sole
purpose of human existence is to kindle
a light in the darkness of mere being."*

— *Carl Jung*

4

Who Am I?

"Our deepest fear is not that we are inadequate. Our deepest fear is that we are powerful beyond measure. It is our light, not our darkness that most frightens us"
— Marianne Williamson

1. Who am I? Write a thoughtful, lengthy response to this question. If you truly saw who you are, who would you see?

2. Have you ever hidden out? Played small? Write about this.

3. Do you have some old issues going on, such as: Guilt? Remorse? Shame?

For example: *As a little girl, I saw myself hiding behind the couch, scared of my father's and mother's anger. As I wrote about that time long ago, I had a visceral experience of great shame: I felt like daddy's little girl, and believed Mom didn't love me because of that – and I felt great shame about it all. Eventually, I put my journal on the bedside table, laid down on my bed and breathed very, very deeply, intensely – for an hour or so. In that span of time, I truly experienced the shame, the fear and the sadness. And so I had a healing with my little child who'd felt so abandoned. I embraced her and brought her back into my life.*

Although this may not be the last recalling of that crucial era in my life, by writing it, then breathing into those feelings, I felt a renewed strength of self-identity. Now I don't have to play so small anymore.

4. Write: What do I need? We often forget or ignore our own needs, so pondering this question will remind you that you do have needs, and that because you haven't examined them, you are not getting them met. For example: Are you the person who always gives loving support to others – but you don't actually get that need met in your own soul? Are you the one who gives encouragement to others, but don't ask for it from your friends? Ponder your needs, and your awareness of who you are will grow.

5. What are you good at?

6. What do you love?

7. What are your gifts?

8. What do you want? (There is a whole chapter on this, so you get really clear.)

9. If you were to speak in public, what would you want people to learn from you? What message would you leave them with? If you were on your death-bed, what big thought would you whisper?

10. What are you afraid of? What payoffs do you get from remaining where you are now? Example: Safety, comfort, addiction to misery?

11. What can you see yourself doing that would excite you and enable you to give your gifts?

12. Write out your values. This will really provide insights into who you are and how you have been acting in your world.

13. Write a poem or story about the person who resides within your skin. Write it with love, and forgiveness.

14. Imagine the perfect life you would like to live.

15. What dreams did you have as a child? Were you planning on becoming a doctor, a lawyer, a teacher, or a mother with lots of children? What were you going to contribute to this world?

16. What have your denied yourself? And what else have you denied that might be going on in your life – something that might be right under your nose?

17. What gives you joy? This is a huge question and when you begin to think about it and write it in your journal you will know what to focus upon in your life.

18. How are you being with your friends?
As I wrote this, I realized that I sometimes don't call friends back right away, so they must think that I don't love them. If I claim that a person is my friend, what is going on within me that might block my love to them?

19. Write about where you are now in your life. State the facts about that. For example: *"I am feeling lonely, and wondering why I have no partner in my life." Or, "I avoid*

going to parties," or *"My finances are not what I thought they would be at my age."* Or, *"I feel like I'm in a dead-end job."* You get the picture. When you discover where you are in your life you can make changes – but not until then.

20. If someone asked you to tell them who you are, what would you say?

21. How do you show love for yourself? How could you "up" the ante? Do you ever take time off? Do you purchase little gifts, like beautiful soap, or a new scarf, or roses for your table? Do you allow yourself to sit and stare out the window? Are you gentle with yourself? If not, why not? How could you change the way you treat yourself?

22. What do you feel about your spirituality? Is it hard for you to express true feelings about it in public? Do you feel secure in your spiritual beliefs? If nobody would ever know some of your doubts, what would you question? How does your spirituality affect the way you live your life?

When you answer these questions honestly, write about them in depth, you will have a clearer picture of your own identity, and your soul will smile.

"The purpose of life is to live it, to taste experience to the utmost, to reach out eagerly and without fear for newer and richer experience."

— *Eleanor Roosevelt*

5

What Has Meaning?

"A life that constricts meaning wounds the soul . . . Only by attending the wounding of the soul, as well as learning to align our choices with its mysterious correctives, can we actively cooperate with this imperious summons to healing."
— James Hollis, Finding Meaning in the Second Half of Life.

*W*ithout meaning in our lives, do we not wander aimlessly and wonder where we are going?

The other morning, feeling a bit weary and overwhelmed, I woke up with that thought: *What has meaning in my life?* So, I wrote about it, and here are some of the ideas that popped into my mind. I hope they will prompt you to journal about what has meaning in your own life.

1. Breathing: This is life. Lying in bed and feeling your breath going in and out. Isn't this number one? *Write about what this means for you.*

2. Love: Loving others, and loving self. In opening our heart to this self, we honor and appreciate her more. We stand strong and allow her uniqueness to emerge. Feeling that love and being conscious of love is food for the soul, nourishment that impels you forward, or at least, sustains you and opens the portal to your core. *Write what you think about this.*

3. Pausing to express what your soul wants to say, so you are in integrity with yourself. *What does your soul want to express today?*

4. Listening to wondrous classical music that epitomizes the expression of soul. Does this ever remind you how you once played piano and loved doing so? It is communion with spirit; simply pausing to really let it in is important. *How does music bring meaning to your life?*

5. When people share their stories, express what has meaning in their lives, are you not reminded to tune in to your own stories and find meaning in them? To *ask, "What was that*

about anyway? What have I learned from this?' True for you? Write about it.

6. Praying with people, or listening closely to them; being an instrument of the Divine. *Do you feel you are an instrument? Journal about it.*

7. Nurturing plants and animals. When you continue to water those geraniums on your porch don't you know that you have contributed to their staying alive? *How does nurturing any life-form give meaning to your life?*

8. Being a light in this world: Treating people kindly, seeing the Divine in them, that they are trying their best to be more fully themselves; smiling and contributing love to their day; shining your light so it brightens someone else's can really gives meaning to your life. *Write about your experiences.*

9. Releasing old grudges. What earthly good do they do anyway? Can you be a light in this world if you withhold love from someone you care about? Perhaps their criticisms have only triggered unhealed aspects within yourself – so those grudges remind you what issues you need to heal. Besides, don't you find that if you're angry with someone, your life

energy feels diminished? *Journal about the times you have released anger or grudges and note how you feel.*

10. Being honest with yourself. If you are not kind, checking the truth about this; doing something about it. Can you remember times you have not been kind, and now wish to be honest and clean the slates? *Write these out.*

11. Cleanliness and beauty in your home. Paying attention to the little things means something because each item represents something about the person you are. If you are too busy to look around your own home, what does that say about you? That you don't look after yourself enough? *Being here on this earth at this time means a lot –so honor that. Journal about this.*

12. Giving thanks has great meaning. When you tune in to gratitude you will get so much clearer about what is meaningful in your life. *Journal about how gratitude gives meaning to you.*

13. Giving your gifts. Have you ever held back from giving what you have to give? It's like hiding presents for loved ones under the bed; all wrapped up, but not giving them. Isn't that

selfish? Giving your gifts has meaning. *Write about the times you have held back your gifts, and write about those times you have truly given them. What were your feelings?*

14. What about tapping into truth. What truly resonates within you that you know in every cell of your being? *Write this and you will 'get' a much stronger knowledge of who you are.*

15. What about being with others who also write and create? Who want to bring forth more of who they truly are? *Write about how your creative buddies, your tribe, contribute to your life.*

16. Family, parents, children, grandchildren – do they not mean a lot to you? *Then, show them they do, and write about them.*

Taking moments to appreciate these meaningful components will remind you that your life is rich indeed.

*"Not all of us can do great things.
But we can do small things with
great love."*

— Mother Teresa

6

Write Letters

"Always do what you are afraid to do."
— *Ralph Waldo Emerson*

1. Write a simple letter to yourself – one where you acknowledge who you are, where you are in your life, the things you like about yourself. Write about your challenges too: as you do, you will come up with answers to get through them.

2. Write a love letter to yourself, and really pour on that love, as if you are the most beloved person you know. You could even mail this. Isn't it fun to receive a love letter? So then, send it to yourself!

3. Write a letter to God – and make a request if you need

to. I do this often and am always stunned when the answers appear so quickly.

4. Write back from God. This is amazing! My life changed when I began to do this. For example:

I will help you through these writings and self-examinations. Writing about them will heal you from inside and you will notice changes in your body, such as improved sleep, or lowering of blood pressure. You have been fighting yourself for too long now. The feelings are "up" for examination and I encourage you to go into them and bring them out. Please trust this process. You are not alone. You will get through the darkness and into the light as you venture in. You will be opening an old closet, cleaning it out, airing it from your psyche – and you will live longer because of this. If it is in you, is it not worth looking at? I suggest, lovingly, that you do. I am with you all the way.

5. Write a letter to a person you are in conflict with. Don't mail it, but simply get out all those feelings.

6. If you're really feeling brave, write that same letter, but put your own name in the salutation. See how you feel. I did

this with a dearly loved person in my life and was astonished to realize that what he had been doing, I was too! So, it was a huge learning. After writing that, I had much more compassion for him – and for myself too.

7. Write out what you feel guilty about. For example: people to whom you owe money. Then, write a letter to yourself and: (a) Plan to make restitution; (b) Let it go; (c) Forgive yourself.

8. Write a letter to your soul. For example: from my 2002 journal, I wrote, then, pinned it up on my wall.

Dear Soul, I hereby commit to your growth. I commit to giving what really nurtures, expands and empowers me.

I hereby commit to listening to my soul over my body, so that I move forward in my life.

I commit to doing what serves my highest purpose – that is, to stay healthy, focused and clear about what is "wheat" or "chaff" – and to choose nourishing "wheat."

I commit to loving myself in ways that show how much I do. If this means letting go of what doesn't serve me, then so I shall.

I choose to have a life that really works. I commit to being a good steward for my life and being the BEST ME possible! With respect, truth and love, Me.

Now, write your own letter from your soul to you.

9. Write a letter to the person you thought you would become – say, the famous songwriter, or the woman who was going to work with Mother Teresa – and explain why you didn't. Maybe there's still a thought that you might incorporate some of those characteristics into your life now?

10. Write a letter from your Future Self to you in this present time. What is your legacy?

All of these letters will help you to get back on the right track, so your soul smiles again.

7

Dialogues

"Turn your wounds into wisdom."
— *Oprah Winfrey*

1. Have a dialogue with a pain in your body. For example: *Recently I had a significant pain in my leg, and as I dialogued with it, I "heard" that my leg wanted me to slow down; feel more compassion for myself. I postponed a trip because of the challenge of it: I knew that I could not walk to the gate of an airport. So, in slowing down, and feeling compassion for myself, I really began to experience more inner peace.* That inner dialogue was so empowering. Write yours.

2. Dialogue with other parts of your body — like your hands, your feet, your legs, etc. As you do, love those aspects and appreciate them. For example: *As I type this out, I look at my*

fingers and realize that they have been working for me for many years – and still going strong. My legs still can do the flutter kick as I swim the crawl, and I am very grateful for them, and for how my body functions well.

3. Dialogue with a former self/persona. In this process, you will begin to release old feelings of negativity towards this younger person, and you will experience more self-love.

4. Dialogue with your inner child. This is an amazing exercise and you will be surprised at what emerges onto the pages. I wrote a whole song about this inner child, and had a huge healing from the experience. The song started out like this:

I look in the mirror for the girl I used to be
And see instead an older face gazing back at me . . .
Where did she go? . . .

5. Dialogue with the older person of yourself, the one who has lived a long time – and you may discover how this person has actually done that. You could thank her for living her life well and ask what tips she would give you at your age now.

6. Dialogue with your stress. What does it feel like in your body? What triggered it? How could you heal it?

7. Dialogue with a great career counselor, therapist or coach. Ask that person questions, such as: "What would be the best thing for me to do?" Then write out what that coach would say to you. It will be really insightful, and will guide you to a next step.

8. Dialogue with your higher Self. For example, here is what I wrote back in 2008...

Me: Feels like I hit a wall. I've been pushing and trying to learn this new "computereez," trying to cram it all in – but hey, there's a lot to do here and I don't seem to have much patience with this woman who has dragged her feet today. Maybe my expectations are too HUGE. Maybe I'm holding myself in some kind of contest here, like keeping up to the boys at the Online Marketing Network, but feeling like I'm falling far behind. Okay Jaya, what do you say? I need help.

Jaya: My child, yes in my eyes you are still a child, particularly when you are feeling this way; out of sorts, like you need your mother's love. And more than that, you seem to feel you're not doing this new business "good enough." Well, by whose measures are you measuring yourself? By whose standards are you setting yourself up to be? By what key points of work are you expecting yourself to be? Do not forget that you are human, that you have other aspects of your life, that you really did have other things to do today – and you did learn a few things.

Me: I still feel stumped and still want to beat myself up.

Jaya: *Be where you are; feel what you feel, but remember that this too shall pass. You are more than those circumstances currently experienced. Trust that.*

But how can I lift up from the heaviness?

Jaya: Let it flow to the top – don't fight it. It has something valuable to tell you. Besides, you are not alone in these feelings. Go for a walk. Breathe in the fresh air. Love yourself despite the heaviness. Give yourself time and space. Pay close attention to all that you are grateful for. Get clearer on your vision. Listen to your soul and allow her voice to be heard. Read something you have written. Be kind to you.

Me: Okay, thank you Jaya, my higher Self. I turn this day over to you now, trusting that you are guiding me.

I recall feeling so much better after that conversation, and then doing what my higher Self suggested. Try it. This process will guide you through any challenges you may be experiencing. It will lead you to the light. And your soul will smile.

"Shoot for the moon.
Even if you miss, you'll land
among the stars."
— *Les Brown*

8

Gifts & Talents

"You've got to appreciate everything.
Realize it as it happens and appreciate it."
— Betty White, May 11/13

1. Write out your gifts and talents: Are you a good cook? Are you an excellent listener? A person who is highly capable of multi-tasking? Are you a great public speaker? You may be a wonderful hostess? Have you ever praised yourself for being a terrific writer? A person who sticks with your task at hand? Someone who is great with animals and they always come to you? A good artist – but you hardly ever tell yourself this. When you write out what you are gifted with, you will feel stronger, walk taller.

2. What do you acknowledge yourself for? Like, do you immediately respond to emails? Are you kind? Have you worked hard on your graduate degree? Are you creative? I wrote from this exercise today and I felt great afterwards. Be specific and your soul will smile.

3. Has a gift ever been a curse? Has it gotten in the way of what your practical self would like to do with your life? *For example, I was always able to leap into the unknown, move miles away, but when I got there I would be miffed, lonely, and shaking my head.* How can you resolve this dilemma? Can you still use your gift?

4. How do you feel if you have put your gift "on hold" – until you retire, until you have more time to create, until you have enough money to live? Sadly, I've heard several individuals in my writing groups talk about this, and I know that their souls are hurting in that postponement process. Does your heart ache from the conflict? How can you balance this? What would make your soul smile?

5. What would you write a book about? Write an outline for that book. Write out ideas that pop into your mind first thing

in the morning, like this book popped into mine. I literally woke up thinking about it, as if it were already written. So, here it is – and you get to read it!

6. Write more about the gifts of writing you could give. *Pretend* you know what to say. If you're stuck on something you need to write, such as a chapter for a book, pretend you know what to say in it. For example: Say, *"If I really knew what to write, what might that be?"* Write whatever comes...

In your journal there is no judgment, so your right brain, the creative side of your brain, just flows with whatever words appear on the pages. Later, read it over and you may be surprised at how much you can use in your actual book or project. I have used this pretend-game often.

7. Ask: Why do I want to write anyway? The following is my journal entry Jan 1st, 2012...

Do I write for myself, as an expression of what is churning within me on a certain day, so I have a record of my life? Or do I write for you, dear reader, who may be experiencing some of these same feelings? That is my ultimate question.

Do I write to heal my soul? To give it the time to express what glimmers from the dark night? Do I write to open a creaky door into the inner recesses of my cave so that I might shed light into more of the stalagmites and stalactites, so anyone with a flashlight could see them? So, it seems I do also write for others – like you, now reading this. I hope you know that the inner workings of your soul, at different stages of life, may be viewed as things of beauty.

I ask questions of my soul that might even upset my equilibrium. Like: What do you really want to do in your life anyway? Being in a certain decade, is there still time to do these things? Can you still dream dreams you once had, or are they shelved somewhere within, so they become a sore arm unable to reach out, or a heavy heart? Are your eyes too sore to read some books that may guide your dreams to function? No! I have lots to share and more time to do it!

Re-reading that journal entry inspired me: I hope it reminds you to write your own message to yourself.

8. How can you best utilize your gifts and talents? Even if you don't earn a lot of money giving them, could you not still give in a smaller way? For example: *A friend of mine,*

a retired MD in Oklahoma, loves to play his horn in small venues. People enjoy hearing him play, and he gets to use that gift. Another friend makes attractive book marks of her poems and gives them to pals. These are win/win situations.

9. Write about the times you have actually given your gifts and how you felt about doing that?

10. What were your most thrilling experiences while giving your gifts? Did you suddenly stand up in a crowd and express your ideas? Did you play the piano for friends? Did you read a poem to an audience? Did you give a meditation to several people and they told you that they "went deeper than any other time?" Remember those experiences and write them.

11. How would you be depriving the world if you don't share your gifts? I was startled when I wrote about this. For example, here are two points that splashed onto the pages in my journal recently...

People would not hear from my higher Self, nor be reminded that they too can tune into wisdom as they connect with their higher Self. If I don't share this, it feels like a selfish thing to do.

If some women believed they were old in their 50's, 60's, 70's, and only trailed their creative gifts behind themselves, languishing in "poor me," rather than feeling jazzed, vital and alive, ah, what a shame. I would be ignoring one of my gifts: reminding women that age doesn't matter, but expressing one's creativity will re-create them. Honoring your spirit is what matters.

Write about your gifts so you can share them. If not, are you turning your back on what you were gifted with? Please don't do that. Commit to sharing your gifts, knowing that just as they were given to you, you will be guided to express and give them. In doing so, your soul will shine brightly.

9

Miracles and Treasures

"There are only two ways to live your life. One is as though nothing is a miracle. The other is as though everything is a miracle." — Albert Einstein.

1. Keep a section for miracles you experience, and the great things that come your way. When you write your miracles you will boost your sense of self-esteem, and realize that you are not living your life alone – but with divine guidance from Universal Energy. For example:

I based a book of mine on miracles that I had written in my journals over the years. It is called, Filled With Light: Miracles and Inspiration for Women. You too can write books from your own journals.

2. Write out the coincidences that seem to happen in your life. Do you envision parking spots and then actually get them? Do you <u>see</u> yourself sitting in the audience of that "sold out" play – then it happens? Write these. And more will come – because you are now more conscious of them.

3. Write about how you feel during a dry financial spell, when suddenly a client or former student announces that they want to work with you. Is this a coincidence – or an answer to a prayer?

4. Write how you feel when someone you love tells you they are seriously ill. Is this person now even more of a treasure to you?

5. Write about a dear friend and how you value them. If there is a glitch with that person, write out ways you could heal this. Then, when you have done so, write an acknowledgment of yourself and your friend.

6. Write about the most wonderful, miraculous experience you have had – and feel the feelings of it as you pen the words.

7. Write out a treasured experience you wish to have. In doing so, your soul will smile.

10

What Do You Like and Want?

"And when you want something all the universe conspires in helping you to achieve it."
— *Paulo Coelho, The Alchemist*

1. What do you like in your life?

2. What do you want in your life? This is a huge question, so ponder it well and write it.

3. What do you know for sure?

4. No matter what age you are, ask yourself this question: What do I want to be when I grow up?

5. Write out your *Bucket List* – what you want to do in life before your transition.

6. What are the blessings in your life?

7. What are you grateful for?

8. What does your soul still yearn for?

9. What do you like about yourself?

10. What do you need to do, to bring forth; to become the person you really see yourself being?

11. What do you need to let go of to be that person?

12. What do you want to spend more time doing?

13. Write to get clarity on where you are going in your life and your business, with activities you want to participate in.

14. Write about the good things going on in your life – e.g. lunching with friends, a letter you wrote and sent. Write about that sweet phone call from an old university pal. Write how you felt when someone acknowledged you.

15. Write out your visions. Be bold and brave and have fun with this. Let yourself be "way out there." Whatever we focus on expands – so focus on what you want, and write it. Your soul will smile.

11

Changes

"If you don't like something, change it. If you can't change it, change your attitude. Don't complain."
— *Maya Angelou*

1. Write out what you might want to change.

2. Write out small steps that you could take to make changes in your life. Then, write out one action you could take. For example: *Go swimming once a week. Clean out one closet. Put casters on that table so you can move it easily. Dust the top shelf of your book case. Give away some books and other things that are cluttering up your home.*

3. Write out the *things* you want to let go of – or, a particular *person*. As we move on in our life, this process is powerful.

Imagine trying to run a mile with a ball and chain around your ankle – well, let it go. And that might also mean letting go of the time spent with some of your acquaintances.

4. Write about the things that pressure you. How you could alleviate some of them? Could you actually see these in a new way, so they are not pressures, but things that could bring you joy?

5. Write about some things you want to improve: For example, *to return phone calls sooner; to make more time for your writing (besides the emails you send to friends); to trust your Writer Within more.*

6. Where is your life diseased? What does not work anymore? Does it sometimes feel broken down, or boring? If you cannot stand it, and if you relate to these questions, write responses and you will get a sense of what you need to change.

7. Write about your addictions. "Who me?" Yep. Are you addicted to misery? Telling your sad story from the past? Or shopping? Or reading till past midnight? Chocolate chip cookies? Maybe you're having one too many glasses of wine? Whatever these old habits are, if you write about them

and own them, you get a clearer picture of what you might wish to change.

8. What have you overcome? When challenges have hit you hard? Have you separated from a partner? How did you feel when your children left the nest? Have you experienced financial ruin? Did you ever fall into poor health? How have you dealt with these issues? As you write these, you may begin to 'get' how strong you are, how flexible, and how well you have coped; how you have transcended these challenges and thrived.

9. Turning points in your life – from where to where? How did you change within that transition?

10. What blocks are you experiencing in moving ahead? What is holding you back from having what you want?

11. What are some payoffs you receive for doing what you're doing – or not doing? This is a hard question, but it will help you see more clearly so you can actually move ahead.

12. Write about a move you are pondering.

13. Write about the homes you have lived in, and what you have gained from each one. Do you have any regrets about leaving any one of them? If so, write those.

14. Write about a change of relationship, or whether you wish to enter into one.

15. What new leaf are you turning over? Will it expand or contract you? Please, let it expand you.

16. What are your positive traits? You need to remember these because they will bolster and give you more energy during the times of your changes.

17. Write how to encourage your soul to smile throughout your changes. For example:
The following always help me…
   *By listening to powerful and moving music.
   *By always writing daily.
   *By reading over books I have written.
   *By acknowledging my higher Self within and trusting her guidance.
   *By reminding myself that I can never allow the ego-gremlin to win over my beautiful soul.

*By noticing more on my walks – like the rhododendron bush in bloom, so beautiful.

*By keeping a more organized desk.

*By acknowledging what I AM doing rather than beating myself up for what I'm not.

*By always listening to myself clearly as to whether I want to be doing whatever I'm doing.

*By accepting my own foibles.

*By honoring that I am a quiet person and don't really like big parties.

18. Write out your own list and your soul will sing through any changes you make.

"Do you want peace? Forgiveness offers it.
Do you want happiness, a quiet mind,
a certainty of purpose, and a sense of worth and
beauty that transcends the world? . . .
All this forgiveness offers you and more."

— A Course in Miracles, Workbook, p. 213

12

Forgiveness

"Without forgiveness life is governed by... an endless cycle of resentment and retaliation." — *Roberto Assagioli*

1. Write about forgiveness – of yourself.

2. There is a saying: *"When you withhold forgiveness, it is like drinking a cup of poison and expecting it to kill the person who hurt you."* Write a forgiveness letter to another person you've held a grudge towards – and release the poison in your own system.

3. Write about an incident when someone mistreats you, or disrespects your property. You can calm yourself as you write the story. Then, write about how you would forgive that person.

4. Write out an experience you feel ashamed of in your life. Next, write how you forgive yourself, and the other person involved too. This heals deeply.

5. *Become* that person you have challenges with – e.g. your mother, brother, whomever. Get inside their skin and write as if you <u>are</u> that person. When you do this, you will understand why they did what they did. It will free you from the negative energy you've been carrying around within your heart, and you will feel much lighter. You will also be able to extend love to that person.

6. Write out how you love and accept yourself and your life now. Notice how your energy increases.

7. Write to forgive yourself for being mean. Remember that time when someone asked for help but you didn't give it? What about that time when you were unkind? Forgive yourself for these experiences which hurt someone else.

8. Write about how you have been healing your heart. Have you found yourself living with injustice, and feeling victimized? Recently, that happened to me – until I realized I was exhausted by all the negativity. So, I wrote about it…

If people want to reside in that realm of injustice then that is their choice – not mine. If I am to be a light in this world, I must clear away any barriers to my being that. Clear away all barriers to being a loving person... If I am so consumed with righteous indignation then how can I be love? I choose to not live like that.

I spent several hours writing, doing forgiveness and opening up to the love within myself. Soon, the sun seemed to be shining and the sky was clear blue.

9. Write the following four tenets of an ancient Hawaiian healing technique in your journal:

"I am sorry."

"I forgive you."

"I love you."

"Thank you."

In Joe Vitale's book, *Zerolimits* (*John Wiley & Sons, Inc., 2007*) he writes with Dr. Ihaleakala Hew Len, about this problem-solving technique called *ho'oponopono*. Practicing this simple process, many criminally insane inmates from the Hawaii State Hospital were healed. Dr. Len did not actually *see* these patients, but would open their files and say these phrases over and over, as if he, himself, were the one needing to be healed.

Through practicing these statements and writing them in my journal, I'm discovering that I love myself more, have released old glitches with people I love, and have experienced a strengthening within. I highly recommend reading Dr. Vitale's life-changing book, *Zerolimits*. Doing the work, saying the tenets out loud, or writing them will soften you, and return you to your center.

10. Tony Robbins says: "*Forgiveness is a gift you give yourself.*" So, spend time with this topic in your journal. It will move you forward to peace. And your soul will surely smile.

11. Dialogue with your higher Self about Forgiveness and notice what comes. For example: from an old journal of mine…

Forgiveness means opening your heart. Listen to your heart and let love direct your course. Yes, you know this is true when tears fill your eyes as they do at this moment. Last evening, with your dear man,, you up-turned a 'root ball' so you could examine it, pick out any worms and set it back again in a more desirable state. Now, the buds can bloom.

Now, the scent of the blooms may waft through your home, and bring smiles to your face. You surrendered to the softness and listened to the strings of a sweet violin play you home.

You have much to learn, dear one. Trusting relationship as your teacher is sometimes difficult for you. Now, it is time to stay open. Your desire to expand any tightness within your psyche is perfect for your enfoldment. Allow. You will write from a deeper place, touch more hearts in ways you may not have been able to. Trust what you are experiencing is opening you to even more of yourself.

As you embrace those disowned aspects of yourself, you will also be able to embrace those other aspects of self 'out there.' They are mirrors. Look into their reflection and see yourself. When you can love what you see, that love will heal you.

I don't particularly like the person I used to be, but I want to understand her, feel more compassion for her.

Hold yourself lovingly while you remember earlier times. You were born to learn lessons for your soul's growth, so what you are seeing now is a part of your lesson. It may

61

not be comfortable, but if you can dive in, embrace who you were, you will find full forgiveness.

I fear getting lost in that time and place.

Do you not know how strong you are? Remember your inner strength because it will carry you through. Never forget that you have your Writer Within with you at all times. Just call upon me and I am always here. Please do not forget that. I am guiding you through this deep process, we are venturing in together. Your heart will be sparkling clean and pure with true forgiveness.

Using this type of dialogue, close your eyes and ask your higher Self to speak with you. See what emerges. You will be delighted with your results – and your soul will smile.

13

Love

"There is a candle in your heart, ready to be kindled.
There is a void in your soul, ready to be filled.
You feel it, don't you?" — *Rumi*

1. Write out: What do you love? Example: Some things I wrote in my journal...

* *To express myself – my Self*
* *Being with my children*
* *Sharing with a friend*
* *Writing in my journal*
* *Watching good movies*
* *Swimming*
* *Hugging dear ones*
* *Nurturing students to open up and share*
* *Reminding people who they truly are.*

Meditating, alone and in a group too.

2. Write what you are passionate about. Example …

*I am passionate about creativity: that everyone is born creative and all we have to do is to recognize that fact and begin to bring it out. I am passionate about inspiring people to tune in and bring forth their own creativity. I love watching them do this in my writing groups. To see them with tears of awe and wonder when they've written a certain piece, to 'get it' that they now know that they can write; this inspires me too…

3. Write about how you are living. For example: *When our former minister at Unity, Glenn Mosley, asked me what size shoe I wear, and I said 7½, he then quipped, "So, how would you feel wearing a 5 ½?* Ah, this was how I was living; too small! But as I wrote about what I am passionate about, I felt my energy soar, and experienced more love within.

4. What do you think of love?

5. How has it affected your life? Here's a poem I wrote after a visit with my family . . .

Love led me through the challenge
Of so many loud voices
Softened my city single stance,
Opened channels within.

I'd forgotten the feel of family,
The embrace that was more than hope.
Now, I can hear the crackle of golden leaves
As I make my new way across the park.

May I fall into grace, remember the joy
Listen and trust this peace within.
Knowing each season is perfect
As I tune in to the Fall in me.

6. What do you feel about love?

7. What breaks your heart? For example:

* A dear friend who is a great actress, bright, always able to remember her lines, is losing her mind. They claim it is short-term memory, but it feels worse than that, when she can't find the frying pan in her kitchen.

Two brothers I know are not communicating: one is blaming the other for a financial mistake; the other wants a relationship but isn't sure how to go about it.

On a worldly perspective, millions of women are still trafficked into slavery – even in America.

Human beings kill each other: For example, in countries like Syria, the leader killed his people, rather than listen to them. Young children were rendered homeless from the killings...

It breaks my heart when people argue for their limitations, that fear paralyses many of us and we choose that over love.

That humans choose to natter and blame, ignore our own greatness, and why we were born.

When we forget we are like waves in the ocean, part of the Great Intelligence; that we belong here. Those break my heart.

Write your own heart-breaks in your journal so you become conscious of what you are feeling about this subject. Doing so will open up more communication within your soul.

8. What if love ruled the world – your world?

9. How can you be more compassionate with Self?

10. What is the greatest love story in your life?

11. Former lovers: Write eulogies to departed love-relationships. It will give you a sense of completion and enable you to move on.

12. Other people you have left behind – like friends, when you moved from one city to another.

13. Write about those you do not want to leave.

14. Do you love your self? How could you love yourself more? What would you need to do or say to yourself?

15. AFFIRM: I am a loving being, no matter what I've done or said, and I deserve to receive love in my life. I forgive myself and let go of any guilt or sadness that would block love.

16. Write a poem or story about love and your soul will smile.

*"Your soul alone has the map of
your future, therefore you can trust
this indirect, oblique side of yourself
. . . it will teach you a kindness of
rhythm in your journey."*

*— John O'Donohue, Anam Cara:
A Book of Celtic Wisdom*

14

Work

"If you don't take risks, you'll have a wasted soul."
— Drew Barrymore

1. What do you like about your work?

2. What do you not like about your work?

3. Is your job your work? Or are you putting in hours only to earn a living?

4. What are other payoffs you might be getting from simply doing a job – and putting off your true work?

5. What would you like your work to be? What are the results you will generate?

6. How could you achieve that?

7. What is the meaning behind this work that you desire? What would you be doing in this chosen field?

8. Are there people you interact with whom you might be more compassionate, kind, or considerate? How could you do this?

9. Is there someone at your work/job who triggers strong reactions of anger, annoyance or irritation? Write about this.

10. What trait in that person reminds you of yourself? If you find one, write about it.

11. Write about how you might resolve this. Could you forgive that person, as well as yourself? See what happens when you do.

12. If you are in a job that isn't your favorite thing, write about how you could improve it.

13. In your work (or job) today, what would make your soul smile?

15

Goals

"No matter who you are, no matter what you did, no matter where you've come from, you can always change; become a better version of yourself." — Madonna.

1. What are your goals?

2. Write out empowering affirmations. Example:

* *I am capable of achieving what I set out to do.*
* *I am successful in my endeavors.*
* *I love my life and my whole journey of success and abundance.*
* *I believe in myself and can do what I intend to do.*
* *My goals empower me. I know I can achieve them.*

3. If single, and seeking a good relationship, write about the qualities you have to offer a mate. Writing this will help you to own more of yourself, and love that person. Hey, even if you're with your partner, when you write out your qualities, you will know how much you have to contribute to your relationship.

4. Write out some things that might get in the way of relationship. For example: Do you like solitude too much? Are you a neat-freak? Do you fear commitment? What are your issues?

5. If you are in a relationship that isn't working, and want to release it, write out what steps you need to take to lovingly complete it.

6. What you envision in relationships.

7. After writing in your journal for awhile, you may start thinking about a blog – so your words touch others. When I asked what I might write in a blog, here is what came...

I could write about a change of energy when getting older, and how one feels about that.

* How it is crucial to open to your creativity.

* How important it is to give yourself rewards for things you have done.

8. How can you step out? Give this some deep thought and write about it. Affirm: *I will not hide my light under a bushel anymore! I intend to step out, let people see me, and really change my life.*

9. Write about where you'd like to be in 6 months.

10. Write about where you'd like to be in one year.

11. Write about where you'd like to be in 5 years.

12. Write about where you'd like to be in 10 years.

13. Write your eulogy – as you hear it said when you are 110 years old. What does your favorite person say about you? What have you done in your life? What is recounted at your time of death? What are the highlights of your life? What are you proud of? What have you accomplished? What is written in the newspaper about you? This will make your soul smile.

Creative Child Wants to Play

She wants to play
I need to pedal back home to work.
She just sits on that old weathered log,
Removes my shoes, scrunches
My bare toes through the sand.

I want to go.
She stands up and walks to the water.
Come on, I have to do my taxes.

She splashes along the water's edge
Goose-bumping my legs.
She doesn't care, just lifts her arms
High overhead and laughs out loud.

What's so funny?
She laughs again
Runs along the cool dark sand, then stops,
Stands on one foot like that blue heron
Basking in the sun.

Ah, what's the hurry?
Taxes? So what?
There's always tomorrow.

Melba Burns, Play Me Muse, Poems on Creativity, 2002

16

Play

"I am not what happened to me,
I am what I choose to become." — Carl Jung.

1. Do you give yourself time to play? How? What do you enjoy doing?

2. What else do you do with your free time?

3. What would you like to learn? Tango? Piano? Join a choir to sing your heart out? Start painting? Take up hiking? Start a book club?

4. What do you love to play? Musical instruments? Tennis? What do you love?

5. Do you love cavorting with your pet? Or a child? Write about that.

6. What brings you great joy?

7. As a child, what did you always want to do? What did you love to play? Baseball? Group games? Skinny-dipping in the lake? Picnicking on a deserted island? Write about these.

8. If you could do anything on your vacation, what would that be?

9. If you do not give yourself time off, why not?

10. What makes you laugh out loud?

11. What do others consider silly, but you love it.

12. What is your favorite movie? Watch it again and write about it.

13. What crazy story would you like to write? So, write it.

14. What form of play would make your soul smile?

15. What makes you <u>feel</u> really good? Write these things, then live them. Your life will change.

*"Do not be satisfied
with the stories that come before you.
Unfold your own myth."*

— *Rumi*

17

Your Story

"There is no greater agony than bearing an untold story inside you." — Maya Angelou.

1. Start to write your own story: e.g. child of which parents. How many siblings in your family? Was there a divorce? What transformations have you had? You can write your story in the 3rd person if you wish to camouflage it when it becomes a book. But write the truth first. Always write the truth.

2. Write about moves you have made, places you have lived, different cities, different homes, etc. This will remind you of who you were *then*.

3. Write about the times you were born into. The era of your birth determines the cultural values of those times, and how your parents brought you up.

4. Write about your mother and father, about their early lives and challenges; how those affected you.

5. What traits do you admire in your grandmother? What characteristics do you love about your dear aunt or uncle? Do you have any of those characteristics?

6. What traits do you recognize within yourself that were from your mother or father?

7. Let yourself travel to places, and to experiences you've had. Write them. For example:

Where might that be right now? Well, to some place warm, where I could walk on a soft sandy beach, perhaps back to Oahu, where my newly-wed husband and I spent two months. I remember swimming in the salty brine of the Pacific Ocean on Christmas day, delighting and marveling that I was there during that frigid season back home in Toronto; wondering where we were going to live; we had no plans exactly, but were doing our best to sort things out. I was now pregnant and soon we wanted a home-base for our child and ourselves. Although we were in paradise our minds were not at peace. Paradise doesn't always bring peace, does it? If anything, it may exacerbate our war within. We were vagabonds then, for a short time, and I felt more peaceful when we finally moved back to freezing Toronto and settled in to a new apartment; happy to walk on Canadian soil once more. But shocked and saddened when my 55 year-old father died there 5 weeks later. Grateful, however, that I was back in the city at that essential time.

It's strange how things work out, isn't it? And it's amazing how we can travel in our minds, particularly when we put our hands on the computer keys and allow our fingers to journey where they may.

Writing that, I felt stronger about reclaiming a major aspect of my own story. You see, penning the pages in your journal lets you take trips, flights of fantasy – and it helps you to recapture past times so you can heal and move on to a stronger future.

8. Write out some of your regrets – and then write how things would be different in your life if you held these in a positive light. What did you learn?

9. Write about a turning point in your life, and how it has gotten you to where you are now.

10. When you write elements of your story, write out your realizations; what did you learn and what patterns did you see throughout your life? What might you want to change now?

11. Writing your story will help you to move on. So, where might that now be? What would you like your story to be from now on?

12. Who have been important characters in your story? Mentors? People you love? People who are no longer here on earth? What would you like to say to them? Write those words. For example:

To my dear friend and mentor, Fred Cogswell . . .

Still in our hearts
Your gifts, your legacies
Reminding us to truly see
Those blue skies and butterflies.

To walk with firm footsteps in the sands of our lives
To see beauty here; not miss it
To pause and ponder and truly be
Aware of where we are.

To breathe it all in
Like elixir for our soul
To drink from the holy chalice of life
Taste and savor it
As if each breath were our last.

I am thankful for his kind support with my writing, and that he published my first book of poetry.

Now, write a poem to a dear soul who has contributed to your life.

13. What is a theme you recognize in your own story? Have you been led by your intellect or emotions? Have you held grievances that have led you to repeat patterns? Write about these.

14. If you could write a new story of your life, how would it look?

15. Today, what would make your soul smile?

18

Creativity

"Words are things. A small drop of ink, falling like dew upon a thought, produces that which makes thousands, perhaps millions, think." — Byron

1. Write about your own creativity: where has it led you? For example: Here's what I wrote in my own journal last February about my creativity:

My creativity led me to Hollywood. Yep, that's right – to Hollywood Blvd and Vine – to a songwriting course. I was out of my element. Sure, I'd written a few songs, but hey, I'd not played the piano at the same time. So, there I was, in a group of (it seemed) professional musicians! And when the teacher asked for my song, I ambled over to the piano, placed my stiff fingers on the keys – and my fingers did not want to move. The song I'd written onto the music sheets was called "You remind me who I am" but I felt disconnected. Sweat was now trickling down my sides and I could smell the stench of fear in it. You know, there's a distinct smell of fear, isn't there? So, I flubbed the piece. There were a few snickers, and when I left the piano, all I saw was the floor. The teacher coughed, and finally said: "Well, you tried I guess... but you need to get it together."

My creativity stopped dead.

I didn't write any songs for a year afterwards!

Now, I am writing again, but it took awhile for my songs to return. Write about where your creativity has led you.

2. Where is your creativity now? Mine is much better now that years have flown by – I have written more in my journals, and have actually put some of my books out into the world. Creativity is like a beautiful, delicate flower and it needs to be tended, nurtured and honored. So write about your own.

3. What would you love to create? A play? A musical? A new song? A beautiful garden? A new painting? Write out your ideas, then visualize them growing and emerging into completed forms.

4. Find something you created – a poem, a song, a story, a book, a painting, whatever – and write how you feel about it now. I just listened to some songs I wrote 15 years ago and loved them. I had given a CD to a couple of people – with very little response – and allowed their dismissal to be *my* dismissal. No more! As I listen to those songs now, I appreciate them; inspired to write more and get them out to the world. I value my creativity.

Here's a poem I found in my journal from 2011…

How poetry comes to me
It keeps me awake at night
When my body craves sinking into oblivion
It holds me enthrall
Like a wild lover
Till I whisper "enough"
Till I turn on the light
Face it head on
Embrace this dark shadow
And love it back.

My soul is really smiling now.

5. In what ways are you creative?

6. What do you love about your creativity?

7. I would let myself be creative if only . . .

8. If I let myself be really creative it would mean that . . .

9. I love my creativity but . . .

10. What I want to say about my creativity is . . .

11. Write something that would make your soul smile today.

12. AFFIRM: I am a creative person and I am now bringing it forth. As I do that, it empowers me to be more than I'd thought I was. I love my creativity. Remember, my creativity never ages.

19

Money

"The writer, when he is also an artist, is someone who admits what others don't dare reveal." — Elia Kazan.

1. Write about what you would do if you won the lottery? What would you do if someone gave you a gift of money, or if you had a lot more cash than you have now?

2. Write out some mistakes you feel you have made with money. Detail them.

3. Write out how you forgive yourself for these.

4. Write out exciting moments with money. For example: How you consolidated your loans and got the creditors off your

back, and how your credit is good now. Or, how you got that promotion at work and a big raise – how thrilled you were.

5. What do you want money for? What can it give you in your life?

6. What were your family's phrases about money? *Money doesn't grow on trees you know. Who do you think you are, expecting money to just be there when you want it? We never have enough to make ends meet . . . etc.*

7. Did you grow up in scarcity? Write about that.
I grew up in scarcity. Interesting that when you break down the word, it says scar-city. Yes, there were scars for everyone after the war because that whole war represented betrayal by the leaders of England, Russia and Germany. Thus, who could anyone trust?

8. Write about something that would bring you pleasure, not scarcity: an item that would give you joy – e.g. a new plant, a lovely new scent for your bath, a table cloth, a new pair of jogging pants, or a beautiful blouse. Does this awaken feelings, such as? *"Oh, I couldn't do that."* Write about it.

9. Write about self-denial, and how that affects your whole life. Do you deny yourself items you would love? How do you feel about that?

10. Did you earn money as a child – e.g. your allowance? Selling newspapers? Working in a five and dime store? Dusting the furniture in your father's furniture store? What did this teach you?

11. If you went to university, how did you pay for it? How do you feel about that? Are you proud of yourself?

12. What do you feel about money now?

13. Have you thought about when you retire, and what you will do about your money? Write it.

14. Can you let yourself have more prosperity?

15. AFFIRM: *I am a money magnet and I deserve to receive great sums of money.* Does this make your soul smile?

*Our lives begin to end the day we
become silent about things that matter."
— Martin Luther King Jr.,
I Have a Dream: Writings and Speeches
That Changed the World*

20

Contributions You'd Like To Make

"Believe you can and you're halfway there."
— Theodore Roosevelt

1. What do you dream about and have never experienced. Give it a try. *"Our duty is to proceed as if the limits to our ability did not exist"* — *Pierre Teilhard de Chardin.*

2. What would you like to teach?

3. Ask: What am I trying to communicate in whatever I write?

4. What are you doing that you don't want to do? How could you change that so you feel you are contributing to your world?

5. What would you like to bless? Or look upon? Whom would you like to touch?

6. Is there somewhere in this whole-wide world you would like to go, to contribute your time?

7. Write out ways you could be more giving.

8. When a collection plate is passed at church, do you contribute? Or pretend that you forgot your check book?

9. Have you heard yourself say, *"I gave at the office?"* Write about that time, and how you felt.

10. What, where, or to whom could you give so it is a win/win?

11. What else could you give besides money?

12. What would you really like to contribute so your life felt more meaningful?

13. What gifts could you contribute that would make your soul smile?

21

Accolades

"Whatever satisfies the soul is truth." — *Walt Whitman*

1. Accolades. We often forget what we have done in our lives, but writing about this topic strengthens the feelings of who we are. What have you accomplished? What awards have you received? What have you been acknowledged for? What do you feel proud of doing in your life?

For example: *When someone asked me this question several years ago, I found myself speaking about the time I spent with my mother when she was in palliative care; it was something I felt really good about. One day, I sang her one of my songs, and she looked at me strangely and said, "You are not like anyone else I know." At first, I took that as criticism, but with a recent shift in my perception, I 'got it' that she was acknowledging me.* As I pondered the experience, I realized that I wanted to write a book about that time – and so I have lots of notes. It's not quite finished, but it touches me to write about it.

2. Write about experiences in your own life where you did something you loved doing, but were never acknowledged for – pat yourself on your back now.

3. Write about things you created and want to do more of.

4. What are you proud of? For example: *When my young son had a terrible dirt-bike accident and his leg was nearly torn off, the doctor wanted to finish the job and amputate his leg. I felt proud of saying, "No, I will not sign that form." One year later he was playing tennis on his high school team. (I have written this story in my book, Filled With Light, Miracles & Inspiration for Women.)*

5. Write about what you acknowledge yourself for doing today. Going to the gym to work out? Making a difficult phone call? Venturing in to a challenging issue and doing your best

to rectify it? You know what I mean. Even very small actions deserve written acknowledgments, don't they?

6. Write from your Writer Within to yourself: For example, here's what I penned from my Writer Within in January, 2012...

Remember, you are loved by the universal soul – God – and so it is right that you do what you set out to do. Many years ago, your goals were defined as wanting to write and inspire others to keep on going. Now, you have more knowledge to do so – and so you shall. But never lose sight of wanting to uplift people – and doing your best to affect the human condition.

What about when I doubt myself and my talent?

Then show how doubt and alienation can be overcome – by opening yourself up – to your Self and to Love. But do remember to take time for aloneness and quiet reflection so you can be the full person you were meant to be.

I 'get it' that I might never know who I truly am without the quiet – and tuning into my own music . . .

Oh Muse, strum me
Play my music
Let it dance its ancient rhythms
Into another's soul
Till we are one
Connected to it all.

I feel your soft power in my belly
And my words and music flow out
Until I remember again
Who I really am . . .

When I write like that, I acknowledge myself for tuning into my Writer Within, for listening, being quiet, and honoring what comes onto the page. I share it to remind you to tune in to your Creative Self/Writer Within.

7. Write about acknowledgements and accolades you would like to receive in the future.

8. What could you do that would make your soul smile – and bring smiles to others too?

22

Gratitude

"Let us be grateful to the people who make us happy; they are the charming gardeners who make our souls blossom."
— *Marcel Proust.*

1. What aspects of your daily life are you most grateful for?

2. Write a whole gratitude journal. What in your whole life are you grateful for?

3. When you wake up in the morning, do you give thanks for another day? Write about this, or why you can't.

4. What God-given gifts are you grateful for?

5. What opens your heart when you ponder that word "gratitude?"

6. When you are drifting into your sleep, what thoughts come to your mind? Are you thankful? Write about these.

7. Are you grateful for where you live? Or what you have in your life? Your fingers and toes? Your physical abilities? Write these.

8. In the midst of challenging circumstances, what might you be grateful for? What are you learning? Are you grateful to still be alive?

9. What friends are you grateful for? Your family? Your partner? Write the qualities of these people that you love and cherish, and feel how thankful you are to have them in your life.

10. What in your physical environment are you most grateful for? Do you have a park close by where you can breathe deeply and walk in anytime you choose? Are you close to coffee shops, places where you can take your notebook and write? Do you have a library nearby? Are the people in your

grocery store kind? Can you easily drive your car to the swimming pool? How are you blessed by the place in which you live? Write these things.

11. Write about near-accidents you might have had – and how grateful you are to be alive.

I remember driving home along the TransCanada Highway in Montreal, pushing it way over the speed-limit on a snowy evening, then suddenly flipping around in an exit and ending up with the car pointing TOWARDS oncoming traffic. With a pounding heart, I shakily turned my Pontiac around and whispered out loud, "Thank you thank you thank you . . ." It slowed me down, and made me eternally grateful for my life.

12. Write about how you have always been protected and guided in ways you cannot explain. I wrote about how I have lived with God/higher Self all my life, and was astonished to rediscover that I have never been alone, but have always been guided. Writing this has helped me to truly reclaim my authentic self. Take some quality time and write how you have been led gently throughout your whole life, with a loving, guiding hand. It will change your perception of who you are.

13. Write about how grateful you are that you made certain decisions that turned you around and pointed you in a new direction.

14. Write about how grateful you are to know how to make your soul smile.

"Cultivate the habit of being grateful for every good thing that comes to you, and to give thanks continuously. And because all things have contributed to your advancement, you should include all things in your gratitude."
— *Ralph Waldo Emerson.*

23

What Will Make Your Soul Smile?

his is a fun exercise. In your journal, ask, "How can I make my soul smile today?" For example . . .

* *To let go and let God. To trust everything is working out for the best.*
* *Smile and let worry go.*
* *To call an old friend just to say Hi.*

What will make your soul smile?

* Commune with your soul. As you value those moments together you will open up to more of whom you truly are.

* Make a date to hear your deep messages from innermost Self. It will enliven you.

* Create a book of *your* soul's journey. As you reflect upon all of your experiences, it will foster your growth in consciousness.

* Examine seasons of your soul, and do your best to fully accept them: Even when winter doesn't feel so good, when you're in depression, when you've suffered a terrible loss, putting your pen on your journal pages will clarify your seasonal moods, capture a picture of your self and illuminate ways where you want to change.

* As you ponder and write what has meaning for you and what you value, those thoughts will guide you to be true to yourself.

* If you are off course, being too extroverted; pulled by others or circumstances, your writing will guide you back to center, and your soul will feel recognized; happy to reconnect.

* Make time to meditate daily. Write from that inner softness and you will be connecting with your soul.

* As you live in the present moment, now, your soul will certainly smile. However, if you are drawn to times past, writing about how you are sorry, forgiving yourself or someone else, loving yourself no matter what, will deepen relationship with soul.

* Love: feeling it, opening your heart to another, listening clearly to another person, loving where you are and who you are, and writing about it will make your soul grin.

* Soul smiles when you feel a true sense of oneness with others in this world; not judging, but knowing they mirror you in some way. Writing about this helps.

* Ask your soul what she wants to say and this will enable you to make direct contact. Ask "How can I make my soul smile today?" Then, write at least a page or two in your journal. Even as you pen the words, you will feel your mouth moving up into a grin. If you remember to do this every day, your life will change, for the better. Enjoy the process. Your soul will smile big-time!

Here is a poem I wrote just before this book went to publication . . .

Listen to the silence in your soul
Listen
Be still
Listen
And you will know

I still my hand on this page
Turn out the lamp
Lie still
And then...
I know

In this silence
My soul is smiling

I hope you enjoyed reading this book; that it has triggered some good thoughts and ideas for you as you write in your journal. You will open up to realms you never knew existed – and your soul will be happy with your communion.

Trust that it is all for your highest good. You will love yourself more, and have even more to offer to our world. We need your light! In this way, you will be contributing to peace on earth.

The End

About the Author . . .

*M*elba Burns, Ph.D. has been writing for over forty years: books of poetry, film scripts, her own TV show, novels, songs, essays and non-fiction books. Her love of creativity has inspired her to express this passion in everything she does. She even wrote her doctoral dissertation on creative thinking; University of Denver, 1983.

"Everyone is creative," she reminds those in her writing groups, which she has led for 25 years, and believes it is crucial to open up to your Writer Within – to persevere with whatever form of creative expression you choose.

Melba enjoys painting, singing, reading good books, lunching with friends, laughing and telling funny stories, movies, swimming, meditating and spending quiet time walking the beach.

She has two sons, a daughter, and three grandchildren. Born in Toronto, she has lived in Calgary, Montreal, Denver, Santa Monica, California, and for the past 28 years has called Vancouver home.

No matter what . . .

please keep on writing in your journal so your soul smiles.

For Further Information:

To order more books, to inquire about writing workshops, speaking engagements, or private coaching, please check out her website: http://www.inspirationwomen.com.

or email melba@inspirationwomen.com

Click on, http://Amazon.com/author/melbaburns for her other books there, both in paperback and on Kindle. Currently, they are:

Romance Your Writer Within and Reawaken Your Passion to Write: ASIN: B00636PZPK

Filled With Purple: Short Stories & Inspiration For Women In Midlife: ASIN: B007XXAET4

Filled With Light: Miracles & Inspiration for Women In Midlife: ASIN: B008K9DYHY.

For two other free books, please go to
http://www.inspirationwomen.com

Made in the USA
Charleston, SC
29 April 2014